Old Portknockie, Findochty and Portessie

Douglas G. Lockhart

A small headland known as Green Castle, the site of a Pictish Fort, provides an ideal vantage point to view Portknockie. The villages in this book have a large number of places of worship and one of these, the low building on the left in Patrol Road, is the Brethren meeting hall. Across the road can be seen the earliest council housing in Admiralty Street which dates from immediately after World War I. Two houses to the right of the council houses, in Seafield Street, have outside stairs visible at the back which gave access to the lofts in which fishermen stored their nets and gear.

Text © Douglas G. Lockhart, 2021.
First published in the United Kingdom, 2021, reprinted 2024
by Stenlake Publishing Ltd.,
54-58 Mill Square,
Catrine, Ayrshire,
KA5 6RD

Telephone: 01290 551122
www.stenlake.co.uk

Printed by P2D,
1 Newlands Road,
Westoning,
MK45 5LD

ISBN 9781840339048

The publishers regret that they cannot supply copies of any pictures featured in this book.

Acknowledgement

I would like to thank the staffs of National Library of Scotland, Edinburgh; National Records of Scotland, Edinburgh; Local Heritage Centre, Elgin Library; Carnegie Library, Ayr; and John Aitken and Sandy Mackie.

Further Reading

The websites and books listed below were used by the author during his research. None of them are available from Stenlake Publishing. Those interested in finding out more are advised to visit the Local Heritage Centre in Elgin Library or the National Library of Scotland which have comprehensive collections of local history books, maps and newspapers.

Anson, P.F., *Fishing Boats and Fisher Folk on the east coast of Scotland*, J.M. Dent, 1930.
Coull, J.R., *The Sea Fisheries of Scotland: A Historical Geography*, John Donald, 1996.
Illingworth, J. (ed.), *Portknockie Heritage Map*, Cullen, Deskford and Portknockie Heritage Group, 2010.
McKean, C., *The District of Moray: An Illustrated Architectural Guide*, RIAS, 1987.
Moray District Council, *Buckie Area Local Plan: Draft Written Statement February 1983*.
Simpson, E., *Discovering Banff, Moray and Nairn*, John Donald, 1992.
Stewart, R., *Sail and Steam*, Moray District Libraries, 1986.
Walker, D.W. and Woodworth, M., *The Buildings of Scotland, Aberdeenshire: North and Moray*, Yale University Press, 2013.
Withrington, D.J. and Grant, I.R. (eds.), *The Statistical Account of Scotland 1791-1799 edited by Sir John Sinclair, vol.16: Banffshire, Moray and Nairnshire*, EP Publishing, 1982.
The New Statistical Account of Scotland, Vol.13: Banff, Elgin and Nairn (1845): www.electricscotland.com/history/statistical/volume13.html
Access to local newspapers before 1914 provided by the British Newspaper Archive: www.britishnewspaperarchive.co.uk
Ordnance Survey maps provided by the National Library of Scotland: https://maps.nls.uk/os/

Introduction

The villages in this book are closely linked to developments in the fishing industry between the seventeenth and the early twentieth century. Portknockie is the oldest, having been established by fishermen from Cullen in 1677. Findochty was founded in 1716 by fishermen from Fraserburgh and Portessie dates from 1727 when fishermen from Findhorn settled there. These communities are situated in the former County of Banff (now Moray) along a four-mile stretch of the shores of the Moray Firth with much of this land on the extensive Seafield estate. Portknockie, Findochty and Portessie share many similar features, with housing in the older areas following the gable end to the sea layout while in the Victorian era new dwellings were built in plots within a grid pattern of parallel streets. In the early years of the twentieth century housing has spilled on to land above the brae in Portessie and along arterial roads in Findochty and Portknockie. Completing the picture are extensive areas of peripheral council housing dating from the inter-war and immediate post-World War II era.

Substantial harbours were built in Portknockie and Findochty in the 1880s. This was a period of transition due to the rundown of local line fishing when steam trawling expanded. As a consequence, communities in Banffshire turned increasingly to herring fishing. The larger sail fishing boats of the late-nineteenth century and steam drifters, which made their appearance in the Edwardian era, made full use of these harbours. The opening of the Coast railway line between Portsoy and Elgin in 1886 and successful exploitation of herring fishing led to a growing population. At Portknockie the increase was from 1,102 in 1881 to 1,560 in 1901 and in Findochty in the same period from 936 to 1,501. Proposals to build a harbour for Portessie at Craigenroan failed to materialise and as a consequence its population remained fairly static.

Portknockie and Findochty are separated from each other by about one and a half miles of farmland. The distance between Findochty and Portessie is similar and land use in this area reflects initiatives by Buckie Town Council to foster leisure and holiday facilities during the 1930s when the market for herring had faltered. An eighteen-hole golf course, the ruins of an open-air swimming pool, a former hotel (Strathlene House) now divided into flats and a caravan site from 1955 are reminders of an era when leisure facilities were created for local people and to attract city dwellers, often from central Scotland, who visited in large numbers before package holidays to the Mediterranean became popular.

The harbours are quiet today compared with 100 years ago when steam drifters and motor boats vied for space. Some inshore fishing continues while the berthing of leisure craft has increased. The decline of maritime industries is reflected in lower populations of which a significant proportion are elderly. Very few local shops remain open, unable to compete with supermarkets in Buckie and other towns and the good road network means that commuting to work is widespread.

THE THREE CREEKS, PORTKNOCKIE.

This postcard of an area called the Three Creeks shows the advantages of Portknockie's site: a flat cliff-top for house building, sheltered natural harbours in clefts in the rock and a place where boats could be drawn up out of the water in the period before large harbours were constructed. The single-storey stone and clay houses in this part of the village are amongst the oldest. The long low building on the far side of the creek was a fish processing plant that later became a cooperage where barrels, used for salt herring exports, were assembled. Rock House, surrounded by the whitewashed wall, was owned by David Slater, master joiner, who became Provost of Portknockie in 1916. He worked tirelessly towards improving the harbour. Nearby is the flagpole used to signal ships in the days before radio communication. Black canvas cones mounted on the pole warned that a storm was imminent.

A hythe is a haven or landing place for boats which were drawn up on the foreshore. This view is from the cooperage on the west side of the Three Creeks. Victoria Street runs south at the point where the track comes up from the under cliff. The streets to the right, Gordon and Seaforth, contain many old single-storey cottages and these too had loft net stores. The track enabled fishermen, sometimes using wheelbarrows, to transport gear to their boats in the Creeks. Two beached boats have their mainmast lowered back into the crutch. The decks had openings and the bases of the masts had pivots to enable this to take place. The masts were placed in this position when drift netting in the fishing grounds. Pulling boats up between seasons was a major task for fishermen and required help from neighbours.

The lack of activity at the boatyard of George Innes and Son at the Three Creeks suggests that this photograph was taken shortly after boat building had ceased. This had been a busy boat yard between 1883 and 1904 when around fifty sail boats were built here. These were mostly Zulus which were 50 to 60 feet in length with tall mainmasts, lug sails and raked sterns. Some smaller luggers and scaffies were also launched from here. Four out of every five boats from this yard were for owners in Portknockie. In 1905 George Innes junior acquired ground at the west end of the harbour and began building steam drifters. The first of these was BF 403 *Parvaim*, built for a local owner, and in all five drifters were built between 1906 and 1908.

This image and the one on page 8 were taken on the same day. Harbours were needed when boats increased in size and number. Local fundraising began in 1882 and, after securing support from the Fishery Board in 1887, Portknockie harbour was officially opened by the Dowager Countess of Seafield on 25 April 1890. Commemorative arches were erected, almost every house was decorated and an eight-foot scale model of a Zulu fishing boat was hung over the main street leading to the harbour. The boats on view are mainly scaffies such as BF 95 *Rosielea*, built in Buckie in 1909 and sold to new owners in Barra two years later. Scaffies at around 30-35 feet keel length were smaller than Zulu sail boats, two of which are moored at the pier. The smallest craft, BF 1177 *Dolly*, was built in Pennan in 1908, had a crew of three men, and was employed in line fishing.

The harbour became one of the most important in the Moray Firth and further improvements were made in 1900 and in the mid 1920s, creating two basins. The inter-war depression and in particular the catastrophic fall in the price of herring, compounded by the widespread loss of gear during a storm in November 1929 during the East Anglian fishing season (the fleet would land fish at Yarmouth and other harbours on that coast), led to a decline in the fortunes of the local fishing fleet. At the beginning of the twentieth century several curing stations lined the western side of the harbour, operated by local interests and by companies from Buckie, Peterhead and Aberdeen. However, the depressed conditions of the 1930s meant that only the Donaldson family of Portknockie continued to operate a curing and cooperage business.

An impressive line-up of Portknockie-owned steam drifters, three of which can be identified: BF 198 *True Vine* closest to the camera was built in Govan in 1907; BF 114 *Mizpah* was older and had been launched from a North Shields yard in 1901; the youngest was BF 284 *Clara Wood*, built in Banff in 1916. The first steam drifter to be built in the Buckie district was launched in 1900 and during the next thirty years upwards of fifty steam drifters used the harbour. Like later Zulus, their hulls were 80-foot carvel planked timber vessels, however beds were needed for the engines, boilers and coal bunkers. The configuration of the stern in their design was changed to accommodate a shaft and propeller. The foremast no longer needed to support huge sails, and so became smaller and was adapted as a derrick to assist in unloading the catch. A wheelhouse provided protection in inclement weather for the helmsman and because the crew was larger more accommodation was needed. Although steam power meant greater operational flexibility these vessels were expensive to purchase and to operate.

The Harbour. Portknockie

This postcard shows the final layout of Portknockie harbour. Peter Anson, who visited in 1929, described it as consisting 'of a north pier about 140 yards in length, stretching in a westerly direction. Two short arms extend south from it, forming, with the two south piers, outer and inner basins.' He noted that Portknockie had 58 steam drifters owned by 555 fishermen. Usually three to five members of the crew owned the vessels and gear and the others had a share in the enterprise. One of these, BF 262 *Lively*, which was built of steel in North Shields in 1903, was first owned by fishermen in Wick and registered as WK 643. Sold to fishermen in Buckie in 1906, *Lively* was requisitioned for wartime service with the Admiralty between 1915 and 1919 and afterwards was purchased by W. Mair and others in Portknockie, who remained her owners until she was scrapped in February 1936.

This photograph captures a variety of boat activity at Portknockie. Steam drifters are tied up in the inner basin. One is displaying its mizzen sail, which provided auxiliary power and steadied the vessel at sea. Meanwhile, two small yawls used in inshore line and creel fishing follow a motor boat into the harbour. The development of small powerful oil engines during World War I led to these being fitted as auxiliary motors in sail boats which gave fishermen a much cheaper method of propulsion than steam. In the inter-war period many owners replaced aging steam drifters with new motor-engine boats. These were cheaper to buy and to operate, required fewer crew members and fuel storage took up less space than the large coal bunkers needed in the steam drifters.

Although postmarked 1960, this final harbour scene was probably photographed around ten years earlier. A hundred years ago Portknockie harbour would have been packed with steam drifters and motor boats. The depression in the 1930s reduced the number of boats and remaining crews gravitated towards the larger ports. As a consequence the harbour was almost abandoned and here only two unidentified motor boats and a handful of inshore craft engaged in creel and mackerel fishing can be seen.

A paddling pool measuring 50 feet by 60 feet was a late addition to holiday amenities in Portknockie when it opened in time for the summer season in 1961. Provost William Mair explained that with the deterioration of the road to Cullen Links it was all the more important to add to the town's holiday attractions. Unfortunately some local people began to wash their dogs in the pool and it was found necessary to appoint a part-time harbourmaster, one of whose duties was to discourage abuse of the pool. The pool is still in use, thanks largely to a group of local volunteers who have raised money to maintain it.

Admiralty Street was located on the eastern outskirts of Portknockie. The southern end of this street, seen here, contains fine examples of typically early-twentieth century housing in a style found throughout this book that reflects the prosperous fishing industry at this time. A high proportion of these were occupied by fishing boat skippers. Carters were another important occupation providing transport for fishing nets to be laid out to dry and of coal between the station and the harbour needed to fuel steam drifters which had by then begun to replace sailing craft. Carters were also contracted as refuse collectors and, judging from the buckets out in the street, a refuse collection was taking place when this photograph was taken.

In July 1919 the town council chose the north end of Admiralty Street for its first council housing scheme, which consisted of eight houses. Water and sewers were already laid, thus reducing construction costs. Houses were completed in March 1922 and were let to tenants soon after. A cart, possibly from a neighbouring farm, can be seen delivering milk. The Buckie area took pride in sourcing a high proportion of its milk supply from farms, which were thought to offer better quality milk than the smaller town diaries that still existed in towns in the North East in the early 1920s.

Until 1873 house numbers were allocated by the Seafield estate in the order that houses were built and there were no street names. The houses were re-numbered by the estate about 1873. Houses built after 1873 have only one set of plot numbers. This practice also applied in Findochty and Portessie and it is possible to find a few houses still displaying their plot number. Shortly after the end of World War I, Portknockie town council had the streets named for the first time and properties were again re-numbered. Since then the names of several streets have changed; Victoria Street in this photograph has become Seafield Street, which can be distinguished from neighbouring streets by the Baptist Hall, built in 1902, which can be seen halfway down the street on the right.

Park Street, at first known as Seafield Street, was developed in the second half of the nineteenth century. Some houses were built before 1873, such as the single-storey thatched cottages in the foreground, while those on the left-hand side are later and were described by Charles McKean in his architectural guide *The District of Moray* as 'a fine line of captains' houses'. The publication of the *Portknockie Heritage Map*, which contains lists of the pre-1873 and post-1873 plot numbers and present day street names and house numbers, is essential reading for anyone researching family history or the way in which the village grew.

PARK STREET, PORTKNOCKIE.   205,323.J.V.

The war memorial is situated at the entrance to the town from the Cullen side at the junction of Park Street and Bridge Street. The memorial was unveiled on Sunday 1 July 1923, a day when the weather was mild, the sea was calm and the visibility across the Moray Firth to the coastline of Sutherland was exceptional. A procession from the harbour led by a piper from the 6th Gordon Highlanders marched through the streets to the site of the memorial, which was unveiled by Lieutenant-Colonel John Bruce Wood, 10th Gordon Highlanders, son of James Wood, a fishcurer of Cullen. The pillar, which is ten feet tall, is divided into four panels which contain the dedication and the names of the 31 soldiers and sailors who fell in World War I and a further 14 soldiers and 12 sailors who lost their lives in World War II. Above the pillar is a carved stone block on which rests a female figure holding a laurel wreath.

Reidhaven Street is the fourth street to be described in this sequence of parallel streets working in a westerly direction from the outskirts at Admiralty Street. It also forms a grid with two more short streets now known as New and Victoria to the west. The name 'Reidhaven' is found widely throughout Banffshire because it has been associated with the Earls of Seafield estate. The 10th Earl was known as Viscount Reidhaven between 1884 and 1888, as is the present heir to the earldom. The majority of the houses here pre-date the revision of plot numbers in 1873 though some replacement of older single-storey properties is also evident.

The location of this photograph is a short distance north of the kirk on Church Street with Blantyre Place in the distance on the left. The straw-thatched cottage at 152 Portknockie (its post-1873 plot number) and the more random layout of housing in the older seatown contrasts sharply with the grid of streets built in the last quarter of the nineteenth century such as Seafield Street (page 16) and Park Street (page 17) which lie to the east of the seatown. Postcards such as this were produced locally, in this case by George Wilson Findlay, chemist, Cullen, for sale to visitors.

Church Street is on the main road (A942) through Portknockie. The merchant's shop and post office on the left is still open as a Spar convenience store. It was built on plot 334 for James Pirie in 1896 who took over the duties of postmaster from his brother Alexander, who had died three years earlier. On the right-hand side of the street is the church hall and beyond that there is a glimpse of the gable of the Church of Scotland which was originally built for the United Presbyterian Church in 1860-61. It was next sold to the Free Church which carried out renovations in 1899, largely funded by a bazaar that raised £237. The scene has not changed greatly since this card was posted in 1910; the only loss is the house standing gable end to the street on the left which has been demolished and replaced by a modern building which contains a café.

The railway line lay behind the houses on the left-hand side of High Street, formerly Station Road. The writer of the message on this postcard gave his address as 307 Station Road and marked his house with a small cross, which can just be seen above the lady on the right in the background. The plot numbers closest to the photographer were generally the highest in Portknockie indicating, along with the house style of substantial two-storey fishing captains' properties, that they date from the early twentieth century. The house number of the writer is now 22 High Street.

This later view of High Street, taken from a similar position as the previous photograph, shows how little had changed in the intervening years. Electric street lighting and telegraph poles have appeared while the communal water tap has gone. On the left-hand side of the street a black storage shed still marks the boundary between the fifth and sixth houses on the left. Further down, the traditional gable-end housing, although distant from the harbour, was adopted to enable houses to be squeezed into the space between the street and the railway station yard to the rear.

These houses on Station Road can be seen on entering Portknockie from Findochty on the A942. The station entrance was on the opposite side of the road. The house on the right-hand side of the street, Morven View, owned by the Donaldson family, fish curers, was the oldest here and the only one recorded on the 1902 Ordnance Survey plan of the village. The others are typical of housing built in the Edwardian period when herring fishing was at its peak.

Portknockie Station was opened by the Great North of Scotland Railway Company in 1886 on the Morayshire Coast Line that linked the existing railway at Portsoy to Elgin. The wooden station building, which was on the eastbound platform, was typical of the smaller stations on this route. The station had a passing loop, a goods siding and two signal cabins though the west box was removed in 1927. The service was typically four trains in each direction and there was no Sunday service. The line was recommended for closure in Dr Beeching's report *The Reshaping of British Railways* and the last trains called on Saturday, 4 May 1968. Track lifting took place during the winter of 1968-69 and part of the track bed on the western side of the station has been used to realign the A942 road. Housing now occupies the station site and only the station house has survived.

This view from the eastbound platform of Portknockie Station highlights the staggered arrangement of the platforms, the limited goods handling facilities and the east signal cabin. In the distance can be seen the low rectangular outline of the school and the first four houses built in King Edward Terrace (page 27). The earliest housing in Haig Street can be seen to the left of the signal cabin. Bungalows, mostly built since the late 1960s, occupy the fields between Haig Street and King Edward Terrace and helped to stem depopulation caused by the declining fortunes of the local fishing industry.

Haig Street is situated between King Edward Terrace and the Coast railway line. The home signal guarding the passing loop is visible. It did not exist when the Ordnance Survey updated local plans in 1902 and by the next revision in 1930 both two-storey houses had been completed and No. 1 Mariner House and two bungalows had been built on the left-hand side of the street. The bungalow on the right, No. 8 Arnish, dates from the 1930s and is where the street ended then. Little had changed in this late 1950s view with an Austin A40 Somerset, which was manufactured between 1952 and 1954, parked outside Mariner House.

A report on Portknockie School, recorded in the school log book on 18 February 1876, noted that: 'The school has suffered from bad premises, overcrowding and frequent changes of teachers.' Later that year, a new school built for Rathven School Board opened on a spacious site on the outskirts. It was described on 1 December as 'well appointed' and its opening provided an opportunity to enforce compulsory education. The log book went on to record that a large number of previously neglected children were now attending classes. Growing population resulted in extensions to the school building in 1892 and 1900.

King Edward Terrace, once known as Slack Road after nearby Slack Burn, was the first street to be developed south of the railway line. In 1902 there were only two properties on the right-hand side of the street: the school house in the foreground, which dates from 1883-84, and the Free Church Manse, which was built in 1890. After the United Free Church joined with the Church of Scotland in 1929 it became the manse of Portknockie North Church. It was surplus to church requirements after the churches in Findochty and Portknockie united and was sold to private owners in 1971. By 1930 two more villas, The Moorings and Aranmore, had been built and by the time this postcard was posted in 1935 one more house had been added. On the opposite side of the street in the distance is the large Edwardian house known as Summerton; this was purchased by David Grant Calder, who came to Portknockie from Macduff and initially had a bakery business in Park Street and in the 1960s owned the village store and post office in Church Street.

BOWLING GREEN AND TENNIS COURT, PORTKNOCKIE.

The depressed conditions in the fishing industry in the early 1930s prompted many town councils to develop amenities that would attract visitors and bring much needed income. Tennis courts opened in Portknockie in 1933 while the bowling green and pavilion followed two years later. The green was officially opened by the Countess of Seafield on 3 July 1935 when she threw the first jack and bowl.

Findochty from Memorial   C 631

There are panoramic views from the War Memorial overlooking much of Findochty. Boat building took place at several locations including the Broad Haven in the foreground. Motor boats and tall-funnelled steam drifters occupy much of the basin with older housing, most of it gable end to the shore, built on the narrow shelf of land below the brae. On the horizon are Edwardian villas and on the extreme right 1930s bungalows climb in single file up the road to the railway station.

The first expansion of Findochty beyond the area next to the Broad Haven took place to the east of the Crooked Hythe and became known as the Newtown. An 1833 plan by the prolific land surveyor George McWilliam of Sherrifston (Moray) shows the parallel rows of houses on the left of the photograph which became Duke Street and Back Street. The Hythe was also the site of James Herd and Thomas Mackenzie's boatyard, seen on the lower left side of the postcard. Herd and Mackenzie came to Findochty in 1903 and 32 steam drifters were built at their yard between 1905 and 1915. After World War I they opened a new yard at Cluny Harbour in Buckie. On the hilltop in the distance can be seen fish hung up to dry to preserve them.

The first houses in New Street in the Newtown had already been built when the Ordnance Survey visited the village in 1866. The construction of the harbour was in 1882-83 and the boom conditions in the herring fishery before World War I were reflected in house building; the street was complete by the time surveyors updated the village plan in 1928. The housing consists of many fine fisher houses and cottages with dormer windows. When originally built, the upper floors were often used to store nets and fishing gear though these have now been converted to living accommodation.

A CORNER OF FINDOCHTY LOOKING TOWARDS THE TRONACH ROCK.

The wild rocky coast between Findochty and Portknockie, a short distance beyond Tronach Rock, the headland in the distance, contrasts sharply with the fine sheltered harbour known as the Broad Haven around which the village first took shape. This view cuts across Sillar Street, a short single row closest to the camera that runs parallel to New Street. Note the high density of the housing and the small yards. The black tarred sheds were used for storage and the tall chimney on the right-hand shed suggests that fish were smoked there.

There are many panoramic postcards of Findochty such as this view taken about 1960 from the path leading to the War Memorial. The older part of the village occupies the low ground closest to the harbour. Later extensions to the latter include the jetty off Sterlochy Street (1901-03) and the south pier (1913-14). By the time of this photograph, the harbour had become much quieter, with only three motor boats and some smaller inshore craft visible. The Hythe which featured on page 30 is the area on the left below the church. In the foreground is the bowling club which was officially opened on 14 July 1937 by George A. Cumming, County Clerk of Banffshire, on the site of the former public school. The horizon features the substantial properties in Blantyre Terrace and Station Road. On the extreme right above the brae are the post office at 21 Station Road, the Masonic Hall built in 1925 for Lodge Bulwark No. 1202 that became the Town Hall after World War II, and one of the new council houses that had recently been built near the 'pre-fabs'.

This photograph was taken from the Findochty war memorial and shows the layout of the three piers that form the harbour. The east and west piers date from 1882-83 and form a breakwater, while the later south pier forms a stilling basin where vessels were berthed. The beached steam drifter is BCK 73 *Burnhaven* which was built by Alexander Hall & Co., Aberdeen, in 1918. Its skipper was William Flett of Castle Street, one of the new streets built at Netherton in the early twentieth century. The postcard caption suggests that its hull was being cleaned, possibly prior to being re-painted. Steam drifters were built in large numbers between 1898 and World War I and replaced Zulu sail boats, though some of the latter were also converted to steam. Steam boats could reach herring shoals more quickly and return to port earlier, thus ensuring that their catches yielded higher prices.

FINDOCHTY FROM THE PIERHEAD

The kirk, on its elevated position on Church Hill overlooking the village and harbour, opened in 1863 as a United Presbyterian (UP) Church and cost £500 to build. Since opening it has been valued as a coastal landmark by fishermen and sailors. The church bell was added in 1887. The UP congregation amalgamated with the Free Church in 1900 and the Church of Scotland in 1929. The building slightly closer to the camera is the church hall.

Findochty railway passengers faced a stiff climb up from the harbourside to reach the station which was half a mile away. After bending to the left, the road reaches the Masonic Hall (Lodge Bulwark No. 1202) which dates from 1925. It was purchased by the Town Council in 1946 and became the Town Hall. A large council housing estate was built after World War II, beginning with forty Arcon 'pre-fabs' which were factory-produced units that could be easily transported and erected. These were intended as a temporary solution to local housing shortages. The *Banffshire Journal* reported on 8 October 1946 that a number of tenants had moved in. However, it was not until 1959 that the Council decided to replace these with permanent houses. The large building in the centre of the photograph is Findochty Methodist Church which opened in March 1916. It cost £1,150 and a bazaar held in December 1913 gave impetus to fundraising. The contract for the joiner work was awarded to local boat builders, Herd and Mackenzie.

This postcard takes in some of the same ground as the view on page 36. However, it highlights the huge amount of new housing on the horizon at Netherton which was built in the Edwardian era. The war memorial on the high ground was unveiled on Sunday 16 April 1922 by Colonel J. G. Fleming of Keith after ex-servicemen, school children and the ladies of the War Work Party marched to the site. The unveiling was followed by a two-minute silence and the laying of wreaths by relatives, and concluded with the sounding of the 'Last Post'. On the lower ground to the left of the memorial can be seen the bowling club on the site of the former public school (see pages 33 and 47).

Station Road climbs up from the harbour and joins Blantyre Terrace which winds round from the kirk. The houses here are among the largest in Findochty and the four closest to the camera were built in the early 1920s. The art deco property at 21 Station Road (Moray View) incorporated a shop and post office after it was sold by George Mair, its builder, when he moved to Aberdeen in 1941. The infant school can be seen behind the nearest house. It opened in time for the new session in 1909 and continued in use until 1969. Afterwards it was used as a hall and library and part of the building was briefly occupied by the Salvation Army in 1982. It had been vacant for around five years when the site was acquired in 1989 by the Grampian Housing Association to build social housing.

Findochty Station was situated on the southern outskirts of the village and consisted of a typical wooden building, cattle loading dock and single goods siding. Opened in 1886, the last passenger service was on Saturday 4 May 1968 when the Coast line from Elgin via Portsoy to Cairnie Junction on the Inverness to Aberdeen line closed. The building was destroyed in a fire in 1975 and houses now occupy the site.

A quartet of sail and motor boats moored adjacent the west quay at Findochty Harbour. Among these is BF 342 Hopeful, which was built by James Main in Findochty in 1901 and was owned throughout its life by members of the Flett family until it was scrapped in 1935. On the right is BF 1091 *Laurel*, which began life as *Pass Away* when launched from the yard of W. R. McIntosh at Ianstown in 1903. This vessel had an auxiliary motor fitted in 1913 and was owned by the Sutherland family. According to local tradition the early settlers in Findochty were Fletts who came from Orkney, Sutherlands from Caithness and Sutherland, and Smiths from Fordyce, Banffshire, and these surnames are dominant in the village.

BF 596 *Benison* was built as a mizzen and lug sail boat at the McIntosh yard in Ianstown in 1901 for James and Joseph Sutherland, 9 Findochty. After James Sutherland became seriously ill, the *Benison* was sold in 1911 to John Sutherland of Blantyre Place, Findochty, who fitted an auxiliary diesel motor. Photographed from Strelochy Street, she is seen leaving the harbour to start fishing in 1924.

In 1914 Findochty was second only to Buckie in the number of fishing boats belonging to it. Although harbour improvements continued after World War I, smaller fishing communities like Findochty and Portknockie lost ground to larger ports such as Buckie. Only a few inshore craft are on view here and the comments written on this card posted in August 1968 were about 'having a nice quiet holiday'. Since then the harbour has been redeveloped with pontoon berths for leisure craft.

In this quiet scene from summer 1907 a yawl makes leisurely progress across the harbour. In the background an unidentified Zulu has just passed the leading light, which was erected in 1903 at the end of the west pier. Some of the oldest housing in Findochty, gable end on to the harbour, can be seen close to the east pier.

As its name might suggest, there were a number of business premises in Commercial Street, including a butcher, baker, a draper, general merchant and a shoemaker. A carter with a typical four-wheeled cart heads up the street. Transport of coal from the station and fishermen's nets provided carters' staple trade. At the rear of the house on the left is a small shed, with characteristic chimney, which was used to smoke fish.

Commercial Street, Findochty

Children probably on their way to the nearby school pass the shop at 2 Commercial Street which in the mid 1920s was owned by Arthur Herd, butcher. He sold the premises to George Slater, chemist, who was also well-known for publishing postcards of the local area. By this time a branch of the North of Scotland Bank had replaced the low cottage seen on the right on page 42.

This view highlights the informal layout of housing in the older part of Findochty. The general merchant's shop in the foreground, which incorporated a sub-post office, was completed in 1884 by Alexander D. D. Mitchell, a native of Craig in Angus who had been schoolmaster at Sandend, east of Cullen. After settling in Findochty in 1872, he successfully lobbied for many public improvements including the water supply, the harbour and the public school. He was succeeded in 1890 by his son William Wait Mitchell, who sadly died in 1907 aged only 37. He was a keen photographer and this scene was taken by him. His widow continued the business and the post office remained here until moving to Station Road in 1941 (see page 38).

The Esplanade, Findochty.

This view is taken from close to the South Pier which dates from 1913-14, when deepening of the harbour and improvements to the quayside created a new basin. In the foreground, dwarfed by steam drifters, is BCK 338 *Onward*, a sail and motor boat built in Cockenzie in 1899 and owned by James Murray of 219 Portessie. It was broken up in December 1925. On the horizon on the right of the photograph are 17 Station Road, owned by James Herd, boatbuilder, and the tall villa at 19, occupied by Isabella Flett, widow of James Geddes, master mariner.

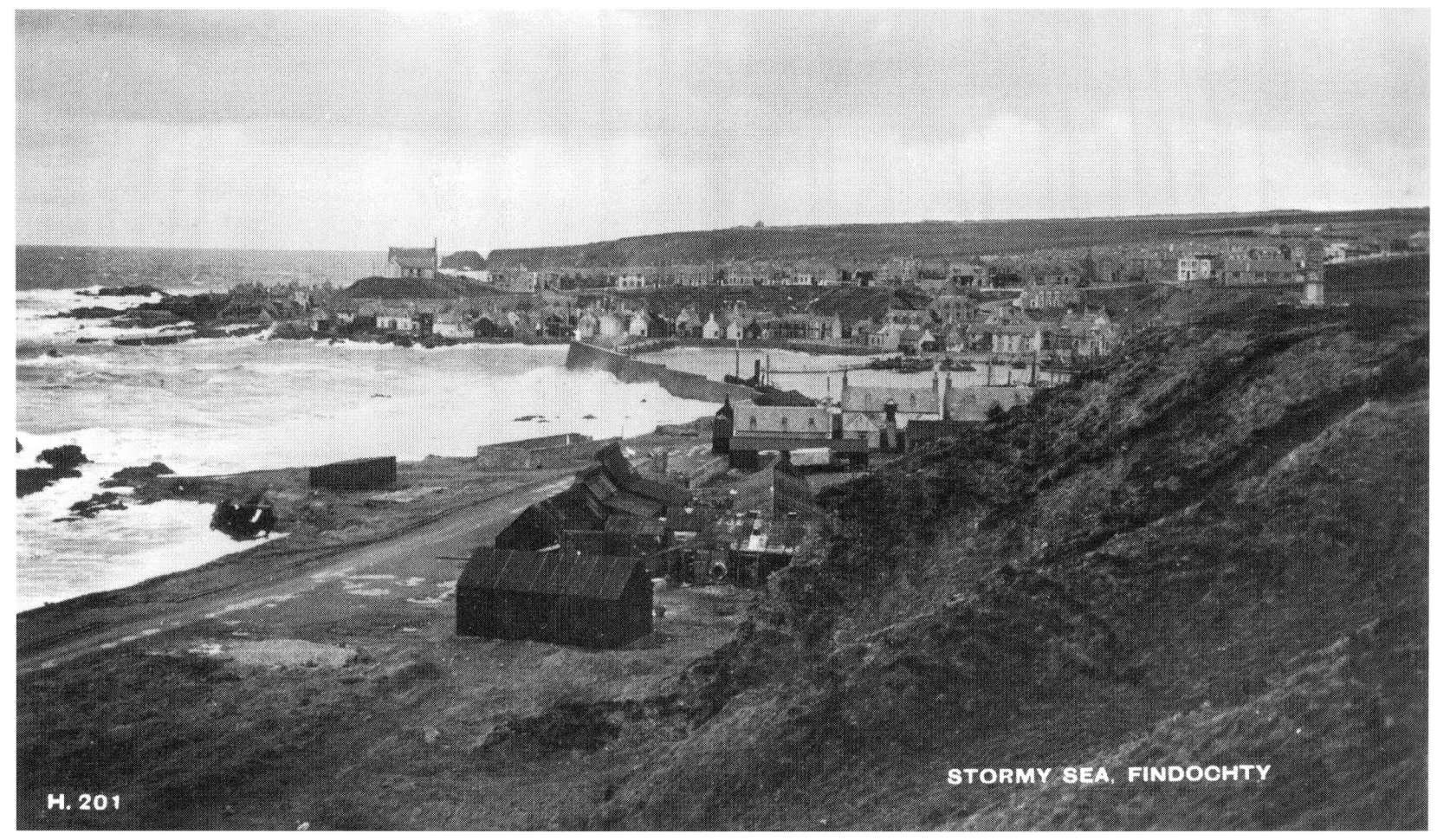

This view was photographed from high ground close to the eastern end of Strathlene golf course and contains a number of important local landmarks: the War Memorial overlooking the harbour, the Town Hall in the distance (visible to the left of the memorial), and the parish kirk on Church Hill. The Edindoune Shore has undergone a number of changes. In 1962 the Seafield estate feued land here to the burgh. Many of the black tarred sheds were removed and the area was levelled to become a caravan site, which is still open. The site became very popular with visitors who enjoyed the fine sea views and the convenient location close to the village.

The school and adjacent schoolhouse were built in 1875. Although much extended in 1884, growing numbers of pupils led to plans for a separate infant school in 1907, which opened two years later on a site off Station Road (see page 38). Unfortunately the school building in this photograph was destroyed in a fire in February 1933 with only the schoolhouse escaping the blaze. As can be seen, the school occupied a cramped site and so a decision was taken to build a new school at Netherton on the western outskirts of Findochty, which opened in time for the new session in 1936. The ruins of the old school were cleared and a bowling green and clubhouse were constructed; these are still there today.

The houses in the foreground are situated on the south side of the main road (Strathlene Road) from Findochty to Portessie. Many houses in the Netherton area were built in the early years of the twentieth century and have names and building dates, a great advantage when tracing house histories: 8 Strathlene Road, closest to the camera, lacks these details, however the short terrace of three properties - The Lea, Roselea and Netherlea - was built in 1903 and the detached house beyond, known as Ashgrove, is dated 1904. Castle Street to the rear also has many houses that date from around this time.

FINDOCHTY CASTLE

Findochty Castle is believed to date from the fifteenth century and was first documented in 1568 when it was transferred from James Ogilvy of Findlater to John Ord. However, a ruling by King James VI returned the castle to the Ogilvy family in 1615. As might be expected the site had natural defences, the castle standing on a rocky outcrop surrounded by marshland. It was already ruinous by the mid-eighteenth century and much of the stone was plundered to build an adjacent farm steading and cottage. In the 1880s the old castle was used as a byre. During construction of new holes at Strathlene golf course in the early 1930s, a human skeleton was discovered by workmen when removing part of the Law Hillock or Gallows Hill, a short distance from the castle.

Strathlene House is situated half a mile east of Portessie. It was built in 1887 by William Gillespie Bryson, factor on the Seafield estates around the time of his retirement. Bryson died in 1906 and ownership passed to his niece Francis Wheen Kynoch, who in turn sold it in 1931 to Buckie Town Council which opened it as a boarding house and tea rooms. Above the brae can be seen the second clubhouse of Buckie (later Strathlene Buckie) Golf Club; this was the former station building in Buckie of the Highland Railway Company's line between Portessie and Keith. It was dismantled, rebuilt and opened to golfers in December 1939.

In a bid to boost the local economy in the early 1930s, Buckie Town Council began to develop amenities that would attract holidaymakers and local people. The open air swimming pool was officially opened by Sir Murdoch McKenzie Wood, MP for Banffshire, on 20 July 1932 and was followed by a swimming gala in aid of Chalmers Hospital, Banff. The pool was very popular until the early 1970s when the opening of an indoor pool in Buckie hastened its closure in 1977. The changing facilities were demolished and the pool was filled in using beach stones.

A caravan site on the Muckle Green was first proposed in 1953. This was only narrowly approved at a meeting of Buckie Town Council because the area was a popular picnic spot and was the only safe play area for children living in Portessie. Seen here around 1960, it was sold by Moray District Council to private owners in 1986 and is still open.

This scene was taken from near Slough Creek, looking east along Great Eastern Road, and again highlights the mix of older single-storey cottages, some of which are built gable-end to the sea, and more modern housing with dormer windows. The black storage sheds along the shore are a feature which has largely disappeared with the declining importance of the fishing industry. There is much of interest above the brae. On the far left is the first clubhouse of Buckie Golf Club; next are a railway goods shed and the rectangular profile of the GNSR station. The shop with the large windows on Station Road was built in 1900 and nearby, enclosed by a stone wall, is the Methodist Church manse. Finally, on the right is Victoria Street, one of several short streets built at the beginning of the twentieth century between the Coast railway line and Chancellor Road, which hugs the top of the brae.

Above: Peterhythe takes its name from another small haven and is around 300 yards west of Slough Hythe (page 55). In contrast to houses next to Slough Hythe, which are arranged gable end to the sea (see the right-hand photograph), the housing in Peterhythe is arranged in four parallel rows between the seashore and the brae. Until 1888 villagers had to carry their water from a large spring which was almost in the centre of Portessie; however, a piped water supply from another spring in Portessie and a cistern were installed, paid for by the estate. The streets were named in 1904 (Findlater Street and Hope Street), though plot numbers for individual houses continued in use for another 20 years.

Right: The location of this photograph is off Portessie's Great Eastern Road at No. 25, the old post office. Putting bait on hooks and unravelling (known as 'reddin') the lines were favourite subjects for photographers. Hand-line fishing, however, was very labour intensive and hard work. Note the beautifully made basket and sculls. The fisherman is wearing a bonnet and gansey (guernsey), typical of the period.

Portessie Fishermen

These Portessie fishermen are resting beside Slough Hythe, which in the early twentieth century was still used by line fishing craft. Slough Hythe was one of two inlets; the other, Peter Hythe, was a short distance to the west. The rock-bounded inlets formed natural harbours and help explain the decision taken by the Laird of Rannes to build houses for fishermen in 1727. The village was at first known as Porteasy.

The Coast line of the Great North of Scotland Railway from Elgin to Buckie and Portsoy opened to goods traffic on 5 April 1886 and a few weeks later to passenger trains. At Portessie it formed a junction with the Highland Railway branch from Keith, which had opened on 1 August 1884. The station building is similar to those at Findochty and Portknockie. Portessie station was popular as a stop with golfers whose course was to the left of the signal cabin and with holidaymakers taking the footpath to Strathlene Sands. The Coast line, like many in the North East, was a victim of the Beeching cuts and the last passenger train called on Saturday evening, 4 May 1968.

Below: This view also looks east towards Findochty. To the right of the bay platform can be seen the tracks of the Highland Railway branch that linked Portessie, Buckie Highland Station and Keith, a water tower, and the two-bay locomotive shed. The line was never a success and services ended in August 1915 with the rails lifted between Buckie and Aultmore. Although re-laid after the conflict had ended, passenger services never resumed and the line closed permanently in 1944.